BUNKER

BUNKER

Stories and Poems from a Nuclear Age

Edited by Daniel Cordle and Sarah Jackson

Five Leaves Publications
www.fiveleaves.co.uk

Bunker
Stories and Poems from a Nuclear Age

Edited by Daniel Cordle and Sarah Jackson

Published in 2024 by Five Leaves,
14a Long Row, Swann's Yard
Nottingham, NG1 2DH
www.fiveleaves.co.uk
www.fiveleavesbookshop.co.uk

ISBN 978-1-915434-23-4

Printed in Great Britain

Contents

List of Photographs

* Photograph by Martine Hamilton Knight
+ Photograph by Daniel Cordle

Introduction

Creativity in a Nuclear Age

When the American novelist, William Faulkner, received the Nobel Prize in Literature at City Hall, Stockholm in December 1950, he worried that the new nuclear age threatened creativity. 'Our tragedy today,' he said in his acceptance speech, 'is a general and universal physical fear so long sustained by now that we can even bear it. There are no longer problems of the spirit. There is only the question: When will I be blown up?'

The world to which Faulkner was speaking was newly nuclear. Five years earlier, the United States had dropped atomic bombs on the Japanese cities of Hiroshima and Nagasaki at the end of the Second World War. In 1949, just a year before Faulkner rose to speak in Sweden, the Soviet Union had tested its first atomic weapon, kick-starting an arms race that would define the Cold War. By the middle of the 1950s hydrogen (fusion) bombs had been developed, many times more powerful than the atomic (fission) weapons used in Japan. No wonder this nuclear world seemed, to Faulkner, like a threat to the traditional subject of literature, which he defined as 'the problems of the human heart in conflict with itself.' How could you write meaningfully about ordinary human existence when the very existence of humans was under threat?

Nearly four decades later, in 1998, the Indian novelist, Arundhati Roy, who had recently won the Booker Prize for her book *The God of Small Things*, responded to similar fears in an acclaimed essay, 'The End of Imagination.' With India and Pakistan trading threats and nuclear tests over the disputed Kashmir region, Roy wrote of a peril so terrible it stymied the very creativity that makes us human. Nuclear war would be the end of imagination not only because it would end humans, but because, even before it started, its terror paralysed the mind.

Yet, both Faulkner and Roy found ways of continuing to think and to write. Literature more broadly, of course, has hardly been constrained by the Bomb.

Nevertheless, in June 2024, when we took a small group of writers into an abandoned nuclear bunker in Nottingham, we wondered how, and even if, literary creativity would flourish in a place so shaped by the worst possibilities our technologies might produce. Although Nottingham War Rooms were built during the Cold War, our age is, too, a nuclear one. Indeed, in recent years there has been a notable and worrying return of aggressive nuclear rhetoric. We wondered, too, about the relation between literary creativity and the very different creative perspective – the brutalist architectural vision – that produced the War Rooms.

Nottingham War Rooms

Architecture is an act of the imagination, conjuring new environments from the mind to turn bricks and wood and concrete into walls and roofs and corridors and rooms. Nottingham War Rooms are a legacy of an early Cold War period in which planners 'thought the unthinkable,' imagining an environment for a world devastated by nuclear attack.

They were constructed in 1952-53 in response to the threat of the atomic bomb. Each of eleven home defence regions acquired war rooms at this time and these, staffed by about fifty people under a regional commissioner, would have liaised with central government in the crisis following atomic attack. By the end of the decade, however, following the development of the hydrogen bomb, the terrifying possibility emerged that contact with central government might be lost or even that central government might cease to exist. Provision was therefore made for Regional Seats of Government (RSGs) that could operate independently. In Nottingham (Region 3) a new structure was built in the early 1960s, enveloping the original war rooms and capable of housing a personnel of about 400 (a manifest for a typical RSG lists 436 staff). In the event of loss of contact with (or destruction of) central government in a nuclear strike, this organisation, with capacity to fulfil essential government functions, would have been headed by a regional commissioner with absolute power.

The original War Rooms were built to be robust against atomic attack. The new RSG building wasn't designed to survive strikes by blast from the new thermonuclear weapons, but to protect against radioactive fallout. Presumably, the intention was that its secrecy would prevent it being a direct target. In 1963, however, the 'Spies for Peace' (a group emerging from other peace organisations, the Campaign for Nuclear Disarmament and the Committee of 100) exposed the existence of RSGs. Their pamphlet, *Danger! Official Secret: RSG 6*, focusing on the Reading RSG (but giving the phone numbers of all the others too!) was sent to the press and widely distributed. The Spies for Peace argued that 'RSG-6 is not a centre for civil defence. It is a centre for <u>military government</u>,' the underscoring indicating just how concerned they were by the possibility of authoritarian dictatorship. Indeed, a striking feature of controversy about civil defence was not just that it addressed the practicalities of surviving (or not) nuclear war, but also the character and accountability of any society that staggered out the other side of it. In his 2013 survey of the Nottingham War Rooms, Mark Bennett of English Heritage suggests that 'the 1960s building [i.e. the RSG] also offers some protection against other threats such as civil insurrection,' indicating that there were anxieties about the cohesion of any remaining society after nuclear war. Suppression of dissent was expected to be draconian.

Nuclear civil defence was controversial during the Cold War and there were debates about its efficacy and about the extent to which it might deter or provoke war. The Historic England official list entry for Nottingham War Rooms comments, 'As the Cold War was essentially an era of bluff and counter-bluff, the illusion of being well prepared for nuclear strike might have been considered as important as the actual preparations themselves.' There was, then, a sense in which civil defence was performative: a theatre to convince one's enemy (and perhaps oneself) that one could survive and that assertions of willingness to use nuclear weapons should thus be taken seriously. Indeed, in *After the Bomb*, the historian Matthew Grant argues that by 1960 civil defence was 'a prop in the [nuclear] deterrent strategy, used to bolster the image of British might, resolve, and preparedness: a strategy aimed at influencing the British public as much as the Kremlin.'

There was also the question of what protection there would be for those outside the government bunkers. Largely, during the Cold War, civilian civil defence was imagined as a DIY effort, focused on the home. Most notoriously, in the 1980s the government's *Protect and Survive* campaign, a pamphlet and films designed for distribution and broadcast in the period preceding nuclear war, were brought to the public's attention through a series of investigative pieces by the *Times* and in an episode ('If the Bomb Drops') of the BBC's Panorama documentary series. A buoyant anti-nuclear movement in the 1980s subjected *Protect and Survive* to much derision. Historian and peace activist E.P. Thompson produced a counter-pamphlet, *Protest and Survive*, arguing that the only defence against nuclear attack was to contest nuclear policy.

Plans for civil defence continued to change and often remained vague and beset by lack of funding. Although they were used for a time as storage, notably by the Ministry of Agriculture, Fisheries and Food (during our visit we discovered materials relating to the 1967 outbreak of Foot and Mouth disease), the War Rooms have lain largely undisturbed. Indeed, Mark Bennett notes that much of the Nottingham site 'survives in remarkable condition, retaining its original 1960 layout and still contains many of its fixtures and fittings. This is a unique and nationally important survival.'

A Creative Archive

The War Rooms are a powerful imaginative space. Although they are not quite a blank space on the map – the most recent

Ordnance Survey map shows them as an unmarked and unremarkable building in the middle of a patch of empty land; earlier maps show them as part of a larger estate listed simply as 'Government Buildings' – there is a void there for the mind to fill. For some locals, this mysterious, austere building in an incongruous patch of wired-off suburban waste ground between housing estates is simply 'The Kremlin.' In entering the bunker, we wanted to capture some of its imaginative power.

We were conscious that we were privileged to access it at a pivotal moment in its history. At the time of writing, plans for the bunker envisage it opening to the community, becoming a space in which a local young people's charity, Base 51, might find a home, and in which there could also be, amongst other things, a café, a restaurant, a recording studio, and a co-working space. There is something heartening about the desire to reimagine this space of seclusion and last redoubt against forces of destruction as an open and creative space in which nurturing and creative human impulses might now find expression.

Nevertheless, we were aware that this was an opportunity to preserve some of its former existence before it enters a new phase of its life. We conceive of our project – and this book – as a 'creative archive,' not simply cataloguing objects and historically delineating the bunker's purpose (vital though those things are) but engaging with the thoughts and feelings the artefacts and spaces of the bunker trigger. After all, the bunker is meaningful because it is imaginatively suggestive. A regional commissioner didn't retreat here as nuclear missiles fell across the United Kingdom, nor did anxious staff in the basement hang up strands of taped information on the hooks of the Tape Relay Centre, detailing the destruction of neighbouring cities. On the top floor, staff grieving their own losses outside the bunker, didn't struggle to identify remaining food stocks and take life-and-death decisions about a desperate surviving population. Yet, the histories that didn't happen – and the nuclear futures that didn't (or have yet to) come to pass – shaped this place, just as, to a greater or lesser extent, they shaped how people outside the bunker thought about the world in which they lived and what it might become. All history is creative to some extent – a turning of what remains known into a story that makes sense – but we sought to supplement more conventional archival work.

The historian Carolyn Steedman writes about archives as having a 'grammatical tense' not of 'the conventional past historic,' but rather the 'syntax of the fairy-tale.' They are places that come alive in the stories they evoke. 'Once upon a time,' we might say, the bunker meant *that*. Or, in the twenty-first century, perhaps, the bunker means not *that* but *this*.

Of course, the imaginative paths our writers trod as they wove their ways through the maze of corridors and staircases, as they paused by the pipes of the Lamson Pneumatic Tube System for delivering message cannisters around the building, or as they remarked on the subtle deadening of sound by the acoustic panelling in the BBC studio, were individual to each. Some were drawn to the fully fitted early 1960s kitchen with its grubby black-and-white chequered floor and the guarantee that sits still in the large unused fridge there. Others found the iron frames of the bunk beds in the dormitories evocative or noted that the regional commissioner's room was the only one with carpeting.

Many were drawn to the systems for communicating within and outside the bunker, and for filing and processing information. The overriding organisational logic of the bunker was, indeed, bureaucratic: the attempt to maintain system and organisation in the face of the ultimate chaos.

We found ourselves discussing the silhouettes left by clocks (now in storage or stolen during past incursions into the bunker) on the walls, and the strange sense of time one gets in there, shut off from the sun and the weather by windowless walls. Other absences also spoke powerfully: tape on the floor marking where walls of cubicle office-bedrooms (now removed because of the asbestos) once stood, broadcasting equipment from the BBC studio, and cutlery from the kitchen drawers. Some elements seemed incongruous, or strangely nostalgic: 'Take Care When Disposing of Smoking Materials' reads one office sign, evoking a world in which it was normal to smoke indoors; decades-old light fittings, their design defamiliarized by the passage of time, seem not ominous but, well, quite cool.

Again and again, our writers responded to the great quantity of writing and documents left in the building. Every room had an inventory, detailing what it held, or what it would hold if the bunker had rapidly to be got ready during the run-up to war. There were, too, door signs and directions, toilet paper with 'Government Property' printed on every sheet, instructions and warranties. A sheet of teletype, seemingly left from a test-run on a printer, repeated over and over the old typist's exercise: 'The quick brown fox jumps over the lazy dog.'

Our writers' work is generically diverse. In one of the pieces, a woman moves into a house in the estate overlooking the bunker and finds herself wandering its corridors in comical but nightmarish dreams. In another, a man is faced with a personal crisis that puts all the talk of hypothetical nuclear wars into perspective. And in a third, someone working in the bunker after nuclear war finds himself developing an unhealthy obsession with a red and particularly soft and inviting chair. These stories and poems reflect, amongst many other things, upon time and memory, on archaeology and the body, on existence and exits, and on all the traces of living matter that persist underground.

As writers, we believe in the value of the Arts and Humanities, and the role they play not only in understanding the world, but in the very experience of being human. Humans are a storytelling species. William Faulkner and Arundhati Roy worried that the threat of nuclear war would impede the imagination and braved their own writing against its horror. In a small way, we hope this collection does something similar: that it tells stories of a nuclear age, but also of an age that is not only nuclear, and in which the day-to-dayness of lived experience, with all its joys and sadnesses, is its own defiance, its own justification: that exploring the world in language is always the beginning, not the end, of imagination.

Daniel Cordle and Sarah Jackson
Nottingham, August 2024

Preparation

Andrew Taylor

For writing about nuclear war:

Lowe Pro BP250 AW III backpack containing: Peter Storm Blisco II insulated gilet, Freedom Trail stowaway trousers, 1 roll of black insulation tape, 1 roll of green and yellow insulation tape, 1 shoelace, 8 x 200mg ibuprofen tablets, 3 x foil emergency blankets, 1 x Body Shop hemp cream, 14 x Hayfever and Allergy tablets, 7 x Nurofen Plus tablets, 1 tin of Original Fisherman's Friend lozenges, Sealy LED3601 torch, Multimat sit mat, 10ml moisturising eye drops, 1 x Nakd Peanut Butter protein bar, 1 x Nature Valley Salted Caramel nut protein bar, an apple, a banana, 1 pack of Belvita Breakfast biscuits, 1 x Juice battery pack, 1 charging cable, 1 x Carhartt Force Extremes boonie hat, 1 x Peter Storm fleece Polar chute neck gaiter, 1 x Moleskine 2023-4 Weekly notebook with photos of loved ones, 1 Bic Cristal pen, 1 x Bic Round Stic pen, 1 x Body Shop Vitamin C SPF 30 cream, 1 x Superdrug SPF 30 moisturising cream, 1 bottle of water and house keys on a ring with a Leatherman Micra multi tool and a brass pill case containing 2 x Nurofen Plus & 6 x 15mg codeine.

For nuclear war:

Drinking water (three and a half gallons), enough food for fourteen days (sugar, jams or other sweet foods, cereals, biscuits, meats, vegetables, fruit and fruit juices, tinned or powdered milk), portable radio and spare batteries, tin opener, bottle opener, cutlery and crockery, warm clothing, bedding, sleeping bag, portable stove and fuel, saucepans, torches with spare bulbs and batteries, candles, matches, tables and chairs, toilet articles, soap, toilet rolls, bucket and plastic bags, changes of clothing, first aid kit (with household medicines and prescribed medicines, aspirins, adhesive dressings, cotton wool bandages, disinfectant, ointment, including 'Vaseline'), box of dry sand, cloths or tissues for wiping plates and utensils, notebook and pencils for messages, brushes, shovels and cleaning materials, rubber or plastic gloves, dustpan and brush, toys and magazines, clock (mechanical) and calendar, containers such as polythene buckets, fitted with covers and improvised seats, polythene bag linings, strong disinfectant, toilet paper, a dustbin, a second dustbin.

Adapted from *Protect and Survive* (HM Stationery Office, 1979)

The Commissioner

Zayneb Allak

It's too late, says the man, we've bought the house.

But I wouldn't have bought it if I'd known, says the woman.

I would, says the man, and we have and that's it, full stop.

He doesn't think the way she does or want what she does but, to him, they are together and that's his last word. To her, it feels like a sentence.

From her bedroom window the building looks like a single storey NCP carpark. It has no view to the outside, not even the slightest gap to peer through, so you have to imagine the interior – you'd guess there'd be some kind of ramp to a deeper level. You could think of it as a square-edged monolith, half-excavated, proof of a lost civilisation from the future. Or you could think of it as a square-edged, Lego submarine emerging from a murky sea, if you wanted a brick-by-brick way to access what was going on beneath the surface. On a windy day, if the grass is long, you can imagine it's surrounded by waves, if you want.

In reality, it's a decommissioned Cold War era nuclear bunker – a huge block of concrete, in something like a playing field, in the middle of an estate of houses that are built where government offices used to be; the people in those houses call it The Kremlin and the only way in is through a dream.

She goes there pretty much every night to meet The Commissioner and keep abreast of the preparations. It's always the same route, lit by a torch beam that reaches one or two steps ahead but no more – beyond that it's cosmic, dark with unknowable edges. She goes out through the front door (that's always half-open), across the road, through the tear in the wire fence, across the grass, through the entrance (the door is heavy, sealing the bunker, but she pushes it open easily), down the stairs and underground into Corridor A. From there The Kremlin burrows from one windowless room to another but it maps itself out in her mind, a blueprint that unfolds as she moves, and that's how she knows where to find The Commissioner tonight.

There has been an attack, he says, it has happened and now you are my second-in-command; in the event that I die you will be first-in-command and I should advise you that I am rather unwell and have something of a temperature, having been caught outside when the bomb dropped and, as a consequence, have only one minute to live; hence, very shortly, you will be The Commissioner; in other words, responsible for government of this region, including making life-or-death decisions about barbarous and unprincipled civilians behaving in anarchic ways, as well as communicating with other regions, should other regions continue to exist.

That's his way of speaking, in long, dominant, paragraph-shaped sentences that nonetheless appear to include all the relevant information. She has noticed, too, that his sentences always assume compliance and tonight is no exception. She will comply, yes, but she will also miss him.

I will miss you, she says, and takes one last look at his face. It's not quite handsome but it is compelling because it's so mobile – it shifts back and forth repeatedly from wolverine to vampiric, animal to undead; she enjoys this repetition because it gives her time to pin down the words – and his mid-century hair is superb, coiffured into snowy peaks that look like a miniature Kilimanjaro. It all disappears in a flash.

She feels that she is hungry and notices that she's in the kitchen. It's big, on an industrial scale, in a Mondrian palette, with work tops and deep sinks and stainless-steel bains-marie and a wide serving hatch to a dining area. Someone has made a shepherd's pie from tinned ingredients but it isn't that bad and she wolfs it. There are people in the dining area, wearing denim boiler suits or grey flannel suits, smoking in between mouthfuls. There is a sign: TAKE CARE WHEN DISPOSING OF SMOKING MATERIALS. She can hear the people talking: at first it's indistinct, as if they're far away, but it gets closer and clearer as she pricks up her ears.

We fully expect to die here, says one person. She thinks this is odd because she has watched several documentaries about nuclear bunkers and the point of them is you don't die.

Die of what? she asks. All kinds of answers blast her and even though she hears them all at once she's able to remember them individually and list them on a piece of paper attached to a clipboard that is handed to her:

> lack (of privacy), lack (of sunlight), deficiencies (vitamin), lack (of power if generator malfunctions),

malfunctions (sundry), claustrophobia, gasping (due to lack of air if air filtration system malfunctions), fright, fear (of being buried alive), hopelessness, porousness (utter, leading to an unlocatable feeling of violation), proximity (to dead bodies), nightmares, not daring (to go outside), medical conditions (diagnosed & undiagnosed pre- & post- submersion), missing (contact, music, the point, going-), lack of food (if containers can't be opened or if food spoils prematurely), cannibalism

It's a long list but by no means exhaustive and she does feel like she's missing something. The laughter beside her confirms that the people are still there but she can't make out what the joke is.

One of the men in grey flannel says to her, may I trouble you for a decision? She is aware that infected bodies from above the surface have entered the bunker, bringing with them their infection. She senses that they are on the stairwell.

Shoot them, she says, and under no circumstances permit them to enter the lower floors. Take care when disposing of smoking materials.

Yes, ma'am, says the man. He gives orders to some of the people in boiler suits and the matter is taken care of. That's how deep underground she is, that's she's able to make these kinds of decisions deftly and with impunity. She notices that it really is quite easy.

Fortunately, she is in her private office. She stubs out her cigarette and sees that she has been smoking and that strata of smoke like ticker tape continue to cross her vision. She blinks. She shuffles some papers on her desk. She has a thought and decides to communicate it via telephone. Fortunately, there is a black, Bakelite telephone under her hand.

Hello? she says. Do you hear me?

Yes, I do, says a voice.

What if, above ground, society has descended into lawlessness? she asks. There is a pause.

Are you suggesting I should go up and look? says the voice.

You, or a junior member of staff, she says.

But, says the voice.

No buts! says the woman. Please report back.

And if I should not return? says the voice.

This time it's the woman who pauses. It really is a conundrum! How can one know from one's bunker if the world above has descended into lawlessness/has been obliterated/is still dangerously radioactive/is safe to go back to? She feels that without answering these questions she cannot return from her dream.

Throughout The Kremlin people are making lists of one kind or another. She feels that, as part of her remit as Commissioner, she ought to oversee this activity. Someone is mapping the bunkers nationally, naming the boundaries of each region. Someone is pinning the features of the local area within the boundary. Someone is alphabetising the corridors. Someone is labelling the rooms and the cubicles in the rooms. Someone is typing a list of every item in every room or cubicle. Someone is typing a list of every moving part in every piece of machinery. Someone is typing a list of equipment needed in the event of unnamed perils above and below ground. Someone is typing a list of the names of the perils. She notes that she is in Corridor K, top floor. She must have come up some stairs.

In the morning she packs a bag with gestures that are only very loosely punctuated: quickly and simply she reaches up and down and wide to gather what she thinks she'll need to survive, such as a tin opener the piano a spade a wide-open road from a wide-open door, and throws them into her bag. She goes to The Kremlin that night for what she knows is the last time, only to find them taking it all apart, dismantling all the cubicles, unhinging all the doors leaning them against the walls shattering all the lists undoing the entire inventory. Everyone is dispersing, even the walls even the building is dispersing. Someone says with a shrug on the way out we were so afraid but look at how you can just collapse it, look at how you can just go.

Peacetime in the War Rooms

Hannah Cooper-Smithson

Had you asked me, I would have said peace
was the colour of light through a leaf

or the sound of rain falling into the sea.
As it happens, peace is the limitation

of signs, tapes, lines, directions to follow –
it is so breathtakingly simple. The silence is replete.

Underground, the world is small.
It is a universe of empty things –

desks without papers, chairs without bodies,
phones without ears.

        In another time, a phone calls under the earth,
         and ribbons spell life and death in lines and dots,

A brace of pneumatic tubes curves upward,
racked like ribs and just as hollow –

there is no pressure, no hiss, no thump of a message
as it shoots from one room

to the next, where dud filaments roll in a layer of dust,
all concrete and glass, with no element of skin.

On the wall, the corona of a missing clock – time remains
an exercise in imagination.

> fluorescent bulbs flare, frantic messages fire
> through the walls, but there is no time –

A hum intrudes: indistinct conversation,
the lonely whistle of a song,

the small, fabric sounds of a body, adjusting.
Silence resumes. Salt leaks out of the walls.

In every corner, a hole, a crack, a tunnel –
light shifts in the distance, but there is no sun.

> only a light that is whiter than bone,
> and a hum, a whistle, a crack.

The red rubber floor is a wound, suppurating,
brittle plaques shatter, peeling apart.

Ribbons of words unspool from the walls
and everything that was tethered comes loose.

> In another time, the wall is warm under your palm,
> but it is night, and there is no sun.

Outside, somewhere, a summer rain is falling.
Outside, somewhere, like a dream – my child.

> In another time, rain is falling. Somebody leaves
> their child on the other side of the door.

Bunkering Down

Anthony Cropper

I was on my way to the doctor's after an urgent call. She'd said it was important I get there as soon as possible. 'I made space this afternoon,' she'd said.

Of course, I already knew what the outcome of the discussion would be. Some news grows slowly within.

It was an autumnal day with just one cloud in the sky that billowed like a threat on the horizon. There'll be storms, I thought, as I trudged along Robin's Wood Road.

I stopped by the gap in the hawthorn and elder hedge as a few cars pulled in through the steel gate. I gazed into the space: a freshly mown field and brutal grey rectangular building. I'd never previously paid it attention. All those times walking past trying to clear my mind and not once had I stopped and peered through those bars.

A handful of cars had parked on the grass and a small group of people were shuffling around a white marquee. It looked like a crime scene and I could hear the mumbles and chatter in the air.

A taxi pulled up beside me and two people got out. A woman with an explosion of bright frizzy hair smiled as our eyes met.

'You here for the tour?' she asked.

The two of them hurried past me and I glanced at that cloud again.

'Yes,' I replied.

The woman stopped, turned and waved, beckoning. For whatever reason, I decided to join them.

As I approached the marquee a man with a clipboard nodded.

'Last one,' he said. 'We're just about to go in. Sam?'

'Yes,' I lied.

He ticked the paper, then continued.

'Welcome to the War Rooms. Our very own nuclear bunker. Privileged access before the developers begin. It's a maze in there so please don't wander off. Once we get inside there's no phone signal, so you won't be able to make contact.'

He was a bright and sparky man, maybe mid-fifties, like me, a time between two ages.

With three floors and no windows, the building didn't appear that big from the outside. Just bare concrete walls and a rusty steel blast door. A new housing development had been built round the edge of the field and after the fallout with my wife I'd moved into a two-bed semi on that very estate.

'Let's make a start and remember, it's not a tourist attraction, it's more like a building site, so be careful,' said the man who was leading the tour.

I wondered who this group of people were, and whether they were all like me, putting off something else in their lives.

The woman with the bright frizzy hair was by my side and she removed a head torch from her rucksack. 'Best own it,' she said. She clicked the light a few times and the flash went on and off in my eyes.

'Trust me, I'm a doctor,' she said, beaming. 'Is this working?'

I stared into the bright white light.

'It's blinding,' I said.

I followed them in through the blast door and we shuffled down a long corridor. The air was dank, still, the walls bare and the floor was coated with fine black dust. We made our way up some stairs. After two flights the narrow corridor opened to a larger-than-expected room and I felt a sudden wave of emotion at the sight of all this contained chaos. I edged in and stayed at the back of the group. The man with the clipboard stood by a builder's light and started speaking again.

'This was the main control centre, the old war room. The whole building could house about four hundred people. All top secret. This was started in the 50s, developed in the 60s and was in use in one way or another up until the late 80s when they finally closed the door for the last time. Before letting anyone in they had to strip away all the asbestos. Notice how the walls have gone from here, just tape on the floor to mark where the rooms were. The developers wanted to keep as much as they could, so all the bits and pieces are still around, though some people got in and stole all the clocks. Why would people want to steal a clock from a bunker?'

People laughed. I joined in.

I gazed around the windowless room; the old doors had been kept but they were now leaning against the bare concrete walls. I remembered the old *Protect and Survive* booklet, and the advice to lean doors against walls and it struck me as ironic that the inside of the nuclear bunker looked like it had been bombed and devastated while the outside world seemed untouched. Strip lights hung from the ceiling, pipes were mangled and disused, and old electronic equipment lay around.

The man continued to speak but my mind was elsewhere. Maybe I should phone the doctor to say I'd be late. Maybe I should have given my wife another chance. Some battles happen on the inside.

'Take your time,' said the man. 'Look around, get a feel for the place, make some notes if you think it will help. Let's have fifteen minutes for you to lean into the space.'

All the other people pulled out jotters and pads. The woman with the headlamp looked at me and smirked.

'Fail to prepare,' she said, jokingly, though I knew there was a deep cut to those words.

People moved around the room. Some prodded at the disused machinery, turning dials that hadn't been moved in decades. Some took seats where they could, a few squatted on the dusty floor, and others settled on old chairs. The room fell eerily silent and I wondered what life would have been like had a siren sounded and the chosen few swarmed inside.

I turned round and stared at the wall. Frayed electric cables sprang like nerves from thin steel piping. Just beside the wires, leaning against the wall, was an old green door, and in off-white letters it said: *Room 33, Pathology*.

My phone buzzed. We did have a signal, after all. I pulled it out and looked at the screen. It was the doctor.

Someone coughed and I glanced around the room at these strangers, their shadows flickering on the walls.

I looked back at that door while my phone continued to buzz. Yes, of course I should have given my wife another chance.

I edged over and squeezed myself in behind the door, just like the advice from *Protect and Survive*. I crouched down in the dust and dark and tried to imagine what it would have been like, four hundred terrified souls wanting but not wanting to hear the news, wishing there could have been some other outcome, some other way through difficult times.

I stared at the phone screen, knowing and not knowing, wanting and not wanting. I pressed *Answer Call*.

That's when the bombs really began to fall.

What You Wore to the Nottingham War Rooms

Ailbhe Darcy

1. NARS Blush

An ormolu of glow from shell-like to shell-like, carcinogenic
parabens, asbestos in the talc, so that your mirror image

might look alive, alive in the bunker, expensive and illuminated,
your head-torch the eye of an icon, diamond-hardened

by pressure, lips victory rouge. These are matters
that appalled your father, the son of a postman, chemistry
    lecturer:

alzheimer's in aluminium foil, microplastics in bottled water,
formaldehyde in his daughter's hair. But there are mirrors

everywhere in here, so you're glad you made yourself up,
alleluia for the golden shimmer, peachy halo, rush of hue.

2. Pockets

Someone foresaw the absence of light, the absence of time,
but no one prepared for the absence of God. You can study

the plans if you like: everywhere mirrors, everywhere clocks,
no chapel, no chaplaincy, no inner sanctum, no sanctuary candle.

Only the hard knots of a rosary you might hide in a pocket,
the secret signs of the cross that return uninvited, vestigial

gestures which inflict themselves, a body's litany
without consent. Like that time in your life you were wildest

and darkest, your world having shrunk to a set of rooms
and a child, a pattern of feedings and naps. Or that time

you *were* a child, in the first confessional box, wayward
and wanting only correction. The slot opened,

nobody met your eyes, and you blushed.
When your father was small – when he was very, very small –

he was frightened the priests would put him in a hole in the wall.
He'd seen it happen to other children.

3. Your green jumper

Glas, from the Old Irish lock or clasp,
implies protection: *is fear glas ná amhras.*

Grey or blue or green: implies understanding
that all of these colours are somehow the same,

the colour of things living and changing.
In here, there's a lot of one and none of the others.

Glas, a sound given by the bells of a ship
to mark the passing of a watch,

a winding up, a conclusion.
(*Glas, sonner le*, sound the death knell.)

Of metal: lustrous, bright, steely.
Of atmosphere: dismal, raw, chilly.

Ghlas, faoi, under lock and key.
Round your finger, the ghost of a ring.

You gave it to a man with a knife soon after
you married. Or, a man who said he had a knife.

4. A Head-Torch, labelled OEX LED

Someone will redevelop this place –
massive smooth grey walls like a limit case

for Brutalist architecture, the suburban new-builds
peeping over to get their eyeful –

someone built it so that when the bomb dropped
someone would live long enough to drop another –

marked each object for its function or maker –
GENT of Leicester; SUPERVENTS of Sidcup, Kent;

NIFE-NEVERFAYLE EMERGENCY UNIT.
First they built it for the blast, then they built it for the fallout,

where Keith never got to be the CONTROLLER,
in his careful suit, all eyes on his tie –

and there is always a Keith, ex-accountant,
who comes for the ultimate sanction,

the taste of metal in his mouth, his teeth grinding at night,
no dentist to tell him it's okay, it's alright –

there are dictations and secretaries, there is the LANSOM
PNEUMATIC DELIVERY SYSTEM –

someone out there will obey your directions or enforce them –
make yourself at home in the studio, the one carpeted

place in the building, the one soft place we might lie,
among serving hatches, filing cabinets, scouring powder.

Later, men in Hazmat suits will scour out the asbestos, but leave
an asbestos blanket, in its packaging, for you to photograph –

to contain each object in a magic circle, a honey-coloured
pool of light, like the syrup from a fallen can of peaches.

5. Wide, comfortable shoes

All the signs said girl: the mornings you ran from the room, belly roiling;
your heart scalded after each meal; how every afternoon you'd beg him
   for froyo –

Let's Spoon, you'd murmur, and he knew what you meant. But now
on your way to the counter, this crone waylays you, an obstacle to your vanilla-

and-whipped-cream-for-the-calcium satisfaction, to point at your middle
and cackle, *It's a boy*. What she doesn't reveal is that you are the boy

and the boy is your father. You'll emerge from the birth reborn, your father's hair,
his skin. Your bones, having moved to make room, are rearranged in ways

that make you more like him. The bunions on your feet are his bunions,
and these feet will never warm up again. When you read to your child

at night you'll remember how, after *The BFG*, your father held your hand
for a long, long time. One morning, your child is crying to be fed. You find

yourself pinned facedown on the bed, immobile, dumb. When
your husband asks, you cannot say what is wrong. It is your father's darkness
the darkness you saw him carry all your life, that holds you down.

6. Expensive dental work

Say this concrete box of silence were a poem,
or better yet, a prayer: the congregation holds
its breath, horsehair in the walls to muffle,
matted and grimy, wayward coughs or shuffles,
the congregation on its knees, *in ainm*
an athar, butterflies dampened by a butterfly damper,
the communion host a disc of sugar paper,
fastened to the roof of the mouth, lips clamped,
we have nowhere to go but in here, outside
there's only the field poppy, the wild primula,
irradiated beyond measure, ash, black rain,
exterminate any insect you encounter, et cetera,
et cetera, and at last the priest is rising
to address us, and we are released, to be seated,
listen and consider, and what the priest declares
is that, in God's world, the cure for a snake is a snake,
the cure for fire is fire, and what the priest sings
is 'There is a Balm in Gilead'. And we say nothing
of course, about being born but in reverse, or
about any of the broken things not in this box.

Room No ..... 150 .....   Department ..... Counter Room.

Item	Quantity	Item	Quantity
Desks	......	Bunks, Two Tier	......
Tables	..7..	Bunks, Three Tier	......
Chairs, Fold Flat	..9..	Blankets	......
Chairs, Easy	......	Pillows	......
Cabinets, Steel L.	......	Pillow-cases	......
Cupboard, Steel C.L.	......	Sheets	......
Cupboard, Steel L.	......	Beds, Camp	......
Tables, Small	......	Bags, Sleeping	......
Cabinets, Wash	......	Mattresses	......
Desk, Typing	......	Couch, Examination	......
Chairs, Typists	......	Safes	......
Trays, Ash	..12..	Screens, folding	......
Trays, Desk	......	Hooks, Hat and Coat	..10..
Baskets or Bins, W.P.	..2..	Cloth, Tabling, yds.	......
Bottles, Water	......	Carpet, Woolcord (Sq. ft.)	......
Tumblers	......	Sanibins	......
Lockers	......	Closets, Elsan	......
Mirrors	......	Cabinets, Map	......
Clocks, Electric	..1..	Boards, Drawing	......
Beds, Single	......	Straight Edge	......
Trays, Pin	..9..	T Square	......
	......		......
	......		......
	......		......
	......		......

Other Items, Machinery etc.

......		......	
......		......	
......		......	
......		......	
......		......	
......		......	
......		......	

Signature .M.A.....O...... .   Checked ....   Date .4.5.67...

Etcetera: Annotations to the Counter Room Inventory (May Day Plus 3)

Daniel Cordle

Every room has an inventory. In the Counter Room, reached by descending the stairs to the basement floor, the white paper mounted on the wall is smudged and browned with dust and dried damp, like an artefact from a dig. It is rucked at the bottom and the left edge is frayed. There is a nail hole at the top. The sheet is hand-typed in Courier. The title is centred and underlined:

<u>North Midland No. 3 Region Nottingham</u>

[we are to understand that this is not the third region in Nottingham, but that Nottingham is the third region in the country, a country that is – we assume – the United Kingdom of Great Britain and Northern Ireland]

[though in what condition we find it, whether indeed it is still a country or whether Nottingham is the *de facto* capital of some nascent, ragged state, is perhaps up for discussion]

Room No..150.. Department.Counter.Room.

[the place of counting and accounting, of tabulating the remains and what remains, a reckoning of what passes across the counter, coming in and going out, so that we may know all that is inside and speculate what remains outside, and so that we may, perhaps, engage in acts of recovery or reproduction]

Two columns, headings underlined, there being no fancy fonts or formatting on your Olivetti:

```
Item                          Quantity

Desks                         ......
```

[not 0 desks, just a double ellipsis, for what is absent cannot definitively be said]

```
Tables                        ..7...
```

[there are, or will be, tables, despite the absence of desks and there are, or will be, seven of them; you may not use the table as a desk]

```
Chairs, Fold Flat             ..9...
```

(*smudged ink, heavy type: **Fold Flat***)

```
Chairs, Easy                  ......
```

[one chair for every table, with two to spare; or you could, I suppose, have three chairs at three tables, leaving four tables for those who must stand through (and for) the end of things; in any case none of the chairs will be easy, the Counter Room not being the place for ease, for the counting of things is a serious business]

```
Cabinets, Steel L.            ......
Cupboard, Steel C.L.          ......
Cupboard, Steel L.            ......
```

(*heavy type, as if bolded: **Steel***)

[why are cabinets plural and cupboards (or a cupboard) singular? as there are none of either, does it matter if they are not there in singular or plural forms? and why does no-one have steel in this situation, for we are counting, we are tabulating what remains, and does this not require some steel?]

```
Tables, Small              ......
```

[it is true that we lack small tables but, as previously noted, we do have seven tables with an indeterminate distribution of chairs around them or perhaps, as the chairs fold flat, stacked conveniently out the way]

```
Cabinets, Wash             ......
Desk, Typing               ......
Chairs, Typists            ......
```

[it appears that one of the things to disappear in the apocalypse is the apostrophe ...]

[... as well, perhaps, as typists, which may be as well for there is nowhere for them to sit and perhaps no 'where' at all; though if there is, against all planning, a typist, they may be permitted to sit on the fold-flat chairs, which are provided, though not on the easy chairs which are not provided, which is as well for a typist on an easy chair is a typist who is not typing, who is not counting, which is the purpose of this room, and if we are not counting, how do we know what remains and how do we know that we remain?]

```
Trays, Ash                ......
```

[dear god, think of the ash but do not tabulate it here – think only of things that can be described as *fewer* rather than *less*; and think of the smoke down here, the lit cigarettes, something to do with your hands to stop them shaking]

```
Trays, Desk               .12...
Baskets or Bins, W.P.     ..2...
```

[paper being the thing whose waste we may contemplate in here and, indeed, paper outside will mostly be ash (see above), so let us keep account of the paper that remains]

```
Bottles, Water            ......
```

[on no account will bottles contain something other than water, say something stronger, for then the counting may go awry, and then where will we be? in any case, there are no bottles of water]

```
Tumblers                  ......
```

[were there water perhaps, there would be tumblers. If there were water / And no tumblers / If there were tumblers / And also water / And water / A tap / A bowl of water upon the seven tables (not small) / If there were the sound of water only]

```
Lockers                   ......
Mirrors                   ......
```

[no mirrors for the people doing the counting, for would you wish to look yourself in the eye when you were counting what remained? mirrors are only in the bedroom of the Regional Commissioner and the office-bedrooms of the Heads of Department on the top floor, for only they can be trusted to look themselves in the eye without flinching]

```
Clocks, Electric          ..1...
```

[if there is only one clock we cannot disagree about the time and we must agree about the time because we are in a place without a sun and we know not how the time passes elsewhere]

```
Beds, Single              ......
```

[one suspects that double beds – and all that would imply – are strongly discouraged; hence, although there are no single beds in the Counter Room, the very possibility of double beds must not enter the minds of the people on the nine chairs of the Counter Room, and so we do not have a line on which to record the absence of double beds that are a terrible distraction from the business of counting]

```
Trays, Pin                ..3...
```
                          (*a larger font, for reasons unknown*)

[three pin trays seem somewhat of an indulgence, pins being quite small; could they not fit in one tray? but we lack both bottles and things other than water to put in them, not to mention the absence of double beds and *all that would imply*, so we are, perhaps, permitted to knock ourselves out with our provision for pins; pins themselves, it is true, are not itemised, but if they are ever added to the list you may keep them in one or all of the trays; if you have different varieties of pin (not exceeding three) you may sort your separate types of pin into your separate trays]

```
Bunks, Two Tier          ......
Bunks, Three Tier        ......
```

[one notes here the detailing of the absence of all types of sleeping equipment, for also missing are Blankets; Pillows; Pillow-cases; Sheets; Beds, Camp; Bags, Sleeping; Mattresses; we are in a world with neither night nor day and what would be missed from the count were we to sleep?]

```
Couch, Examination       ......
```
                    (*again, the heavy type: **Examination***)
```
Safe                     ......
```

[this being a place of safety, the safes are not needed]

```
Screens, folding         ......
```
                (*the lower case 'f' is, one assumes, an error*)
```
Hooks, Hat and Coat      ..10..
```

[we are well provisioned with things on which to hang your outer garments should you decide to pop outside, maybe to replenish your stock of pins; you can retrieve your hats and coats from the hooks provided and return them on your return, should you return]

[should you return?]

And then there are the other things whose absence is recorded:

```
Cloth, Tabling, yds.; Carpet,
Woolcord (Sq. ft); Sanibins;
Closets, Elsan; Cabinets, Map;
Boards, Drawing; Straight Edge; T
Square
```

[hard floors being easier to wipe clean than carpet of the fluids of the body]

And finally there are the things whose absence is not recorded, all those things in the universe that we simply designate under the labels:

```
Other Items, Machinery etc.
```

[there is much, as the sirens sound and the heavy latches secure the steel blast doors, as we scramble down the concrete stairs and look nervously one to the other, that will not pass across the counter and that will thus go uncounted; let everything in the world outside the doors, those things we endeavour not to count as we tabulate our folding chairs and avoid looking at our eyes in the absent mirrors, be designated simply as *etcetera*]

Signed (but not checked) on this 4th day of May, 1967

The Boulder

Jonathan Hogg

The bodies will cover the books, if it comes to the final violence. The bodies will have their revenge on the novels which left them out.

—Maggie Gee, *The Burning Book* (1983)

The Nottingham War Rooms lie half-wedged underground, like a boulder thrown into sand. From afar, surrounded by arid-looking wasteland, the structure appears nondescript, but it is a remnant of the infrastructure of nuclear deterrence: a monument to old nuclear fear.

A large metal door is partly hidden behind a thick line of dark green conifer trees, planted in an attempt to obscure or naturalise the bunker, or to manufacture disconnection from the world. As they grew, so did suppression of the ultimate rationale for the bunker: the possibility of total war carried to its logical conclusion. Had a nuclear weapon hit Nottingham, these trees would have been incinerated, perhaps surviving only in white blast shadows cast on the bunker's concrete walls.

Now, the bunker is a relic of old plans for the final violence. A temporary attempt to survive, a space from which to imagine a post-nuclear future, it has taken on a geologic quality, as if hewn from rock.

As we go through the door, the air turns musty and cool, the darkness expanding through a maze of corridors. Where light does appear intermittently from stark-white tubes, specks of dust shine, suspended. Down a corridor that smells of laundry powder, something has dissolved through wooden shelving, splintering and twisting the wood into plumes of curved feathers.

Everything in the War Rooms is man-made and regulated, shaped by a beige dream of order. But in the decay, familiar objects are made strange. In the offices, circular shadows high on the walls show where clocks once offered a measure of time. In the bathrooms, there are footprints and finger smudges in the dust. In the Tape Relay Centre, discarded paper is scattered on the floor, words obscured by grime. This is not a comforting sanctum or den: it is a dereliction.

Deep in the still coldness of its interior, the abandoned bunker at first appears to be defined by the absence of human contact – an architectural, even archaeological, ruin. Yet it slowly reveals itself as having, or being, a body, the pipes of the air-tube communication system running through it like veins, and the silent engine in the plant room a heart poised to beat against the final violence, struggling to sustain the lives of its imagined inhabitants. Half-buried in the land and in memory, this body holds imperfect histories in which the lives that shaped and built it – and that were destined for it in some projected nuclear future – are increasingly forgotten.

As we return to the entrance, the world outside comes back into focus: a new brightness and a warmer air fills the lungs. The bunker was only ever a temporary attempt to survive, to plan, to organise and to connect to the future, but in spite of itself it has a solidity to its foundations, a lithic permanence to its walls. This Regional Seat of Government has opened its doors, but our connectedness with it is mediated still by hesitant steps, cautious descents into the bunkers of the imagination where our fascination with, and fear of, the final violence play out.

Regeneration Condo

Philip Leonard

Ventilation fans carve air into shapes that can be felt but not seen. An illusion of breeze. He picks at a fragment of paint flaking from the wall. Splinters penetrate the soft bed under his fingernail, Navajo white blending with carmine. He remembers the advert.

Where will you go when disaster strikes?

A small drop of blood pools at the end of his finger. He checks the feed from the security camera. The guard who tried to get into their apartment is still there, tilting uneasily against the door.

They weren't escaping disaster, he reminds himself, and this was never about hiding in a bunker. Something greater was happening here – they had talked about it often.

'We can still be the creators of a new earth,' he says.

'Overachievers in the underground,' she replies.

'This isn't just survival.'

'A new society. A renewed world. This is still our mantra.'

They wouldn't run out of power or food or water, they'd been told. Their retreat wouldn't decay, it'd last for centuries.

Forget starting again on Mars. Forget an island in Fiji. Choose subterranea. Choose an incubator of the future. Choose rebirth. Think of the freedom you'll have!

Rust punctuates the apartment door. An ellipsis, she thinks, an exclamation mark. Walls mumble and stutter, the floor was becoming brittled and tortiled.

'Like walking on nachos,' he says.

'Or scabs,' she adds.

A fortified seclusion for the visionaries. Your safety is guaranteed!

He looks again at the image from the other side of the door. The guard is still there, but slumped and motionless, features no longer readable.

He runs a finger through the dust. 'We're still in control,' he tells her, pointing at the screen. 'That's what leadership down here looks like.'

Eclogue

Jay Gao

After '1mt Airburst' in *Nottingham After the Bomb* (1983)

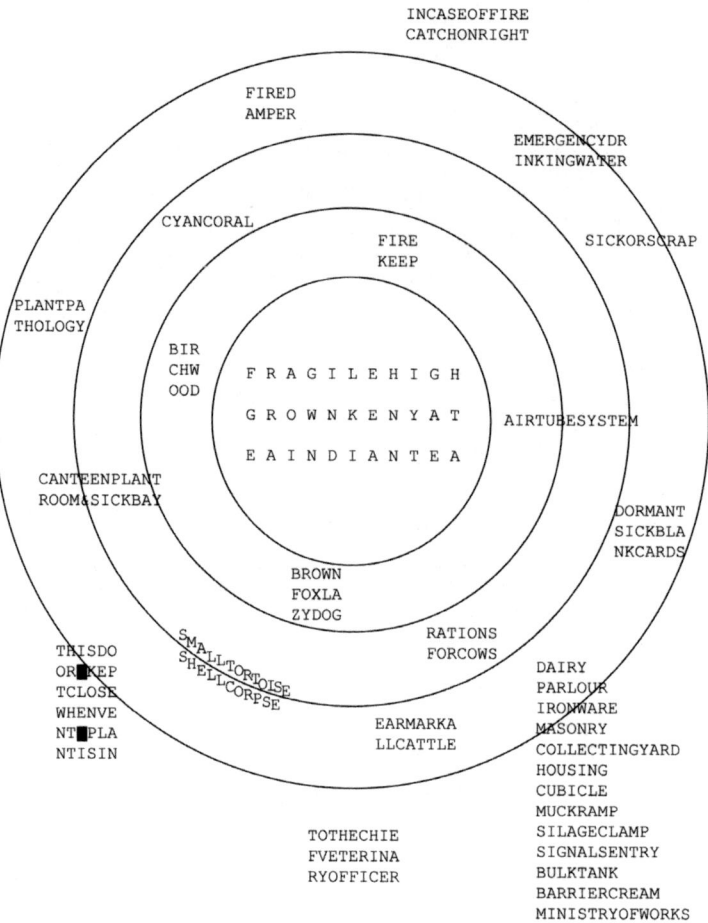

Catalogue

Jay Gao

After '1mt Airburst' in *Nottingham After the Bomb* (1983)

```
DESKS (CONCENTRIC)
TABLES (OF █████)
CHAIRS (ILLEGIBLE)
CHAIRS (EASY)
CABINETS (STEEL)
CUPBOARD (STEEL)
CUPBOARD (CONCRETE)
CUPBOARD (YEAST AND MOLASSES WILL KEEP YOU W██)
TABLES
CABINETS (DISINFECTING POW██)
DESK (TYPING)
CHAIRS (TYPISTS)
TYPISTS (SPARES)
TRAYS (ACOUSTIC ASH (TREE))
TRAYS (TEST PHASE)
BASKETS OR BINS (CERTAIN ACTION IN CERTAIN EMERGENCIES)
BOTTLES (WATER)
BOTTLES (WATER (VULCANISED (CORAL-LIKE)))
BOTTLES (TOXIC)
TUMBLERS
LOCKERS
MIRRORS (BOO! BEHIND YOU!)
CLOCKS (ELECTRIC (MASTER (NOT TO EE USED)))
CLOCKS (CIVIL DEFENCE)
BEDS (HOUSING ESTATE)
BUNKS (FIVE TIER (FALLOUT RISK))
BUNKS (FOUR TIER)
BUNKS (THREE TIER)
BUNKS (TWO TIER)
BLANKETS
PILLOWS (ASBESTOS)
PILLOW-CASES (SCARRED █)
SHEETS (DOWNWIND)
SHEETS (LICHEN)
BEDS (SICK ROOM)
BAGS (FOR MEMORY)
MATTRESSES (A CONCRETE APRON)
COUCH (EXAMINATION)
SANIBINS (TAKE CARE WHEN DISPOSING OF SM█ MATERIALS)
CLOSETS (ARCHIVES)
CABINETS (MAPS OF NOT████████████STAN)
MAPS (CABINETS OF RUINS)
BOARDS (PARTICLES)
STRAIGHT EDGE (THE RAIN)
T SQUARE (SOME LIMITS (WASTEGROUND))
OTHER ITEMS, MACHINERY ETC. (COMMONPLACE)
OTHER ITEMS, MACHINERY ETC. (█LESS TIME)
```

A Long Time

Maria Gil Ulldemolins

He was staring at the chair. He knew that was the right way to put it. He wanted to say the chair was staring at him. But it was not. Of course. The chair was not staring at him. He was the one doing the staring. He had been staring at the chair for a long time. Or, at least, everything felt like a long time, lately. Lately, too, was itself a long time.

He had heard that there was horsehair in the ceiling. All that reinforced concrete, the thickness of it. But somehow it still needed horsehair for extra insulation (and insulation was, admittedly, rather important). He assumed horsehair came from manes and tails. Long, expressive. It needed fields, this image. Plenty of green, a perennial spring (although he knew better than that). Imagining something once wild woven into the bunker made him feel both very sad and understood. Protected, even. He knew better than naming hope, though. Lately, he realised he had been layering his feelings like this, like building materials. Contradictions, soft and unspoken. Intimate confusions. Lately, it had been a long time.

The chair would never have been remarkable in the before-times. A simple office thing. Red. The colour was pretty, true. He had never thought of pretty colours, before. How circumstances change you. But he did not think about the before. That was on purpose. Discipline was necessary, here. *Before* was behind the thick steel blast door. He would feel a pull every time he passed it. But that was nonsense. *Before* was elsewhere. Except that it wasn't there anymore either, of course. *Before* was a long time ago.

The jacket of the uniform his father wore had had some interlining made of horsehair, too. He had only ever known the uniform as a kind of corpse hanging in the closet. Present in the room even when the closet door was shut. Something that was his father, but also was not. Once-alive. Once-animal. Shaped into obedience as if by a bridle or whip.

The chair was plain. It had no decorative whimsy. Nothing here did, really. A numbed craving arose from the pit of his stomach, something like the gleam of a mercury glass ornament on a Christmas tree. He put down the memory. That was unhelpful behaviour. He focused instead on the chair. Plush, but shallow. Comfortable, but not indulgent. No, she would not be indulgent. It. It would not be indulgent. The red chair. The red chair softly padded on the arms and seats. Open, welcoming. He stopped the word 'expectant' from forming in his mind.

A structural matter, horsehair. Stiff yet supple. A special thing. Honourable, even. It does not knot, but it does bend to will. Hence its use in upholstery, violin bows, shaving brushes, even plaster. Sometimes you can push a metaphor too far. But if you only inherit the material, dumb fact of it, and none of its knowledge, you are safe. No risk of overdoing it, then.

The thing about the chair was that it was slightly battered. She, too, was of service. It. It, too, was of service. The pretty red textile was worn. No sun discolouration, mind you, there being no sun, here. Just some wear and tear. Things to be expected. The fabric edges of the arms were thinning. The top right of the backrest was beginning to hang. It draped a little. A coquettish gesture here, of all places. He had not thought of draping and soft signals in a long, long time.

He did not know, because he had never been told. There are things your parents do not tell you. All the better for it, really. He did not know that his mother had worn the jacket the night he was conceived. Once, she had had a bit too much sherry and mentioned a party, how she knew it was that night that it happened. It took him by surprise, back then, the thought of a party, sitting in his parents' small, dark living room. She did not offer more, waving away what she had just said, cheeks flushed. He could smell his mother's perfume, for a second, soapy and powdery, mixed with the decades of cigarette smoke steeped in the wallpaper. He understood about the festive mood, the drinks, the guests gone but the alcohol lingering, about being young. But he would have never guessed about the uniform jacket. About how its lining might feel on bare skin. About its shoulders being so much wider than his mother's.

He had stretched a finger and was caressing the hard frame of the chair. A thoughtless movement. He took a step back. It had been a really long time.

He had a wife, once. Out there, in the before. He had buried her memory so deep inside himself that she did not even appear clearly in dreams. When he woke up in a wet jolt, all he could see was a daze of abstract skin. It was important he never ever remembered her face. Her eyes, in particular. Her eyes the day he told her. The white, silent width of them. He may have allowed for some sentimentality regarding the nape of her neck, if it came to it. Her turned head and the way the collar of her dress barely touched her. She had refused to watch him leave. He never thought about any of this long enough to feel the nuclear blast of guilt. She would have been much better in a crisis than him. She was practical, economical of movements, precise. He imagined her waiting, sitting straight, adjusting the front of the cardigan just so, dry fingers flat against the wool. He halted the thought. That was so long ago, it was as if it had never happened.

The thing about this place was that you were one of many. That required coordination, ant-like activity. They watched out for each other. Which meant they were always watching each other, too. They very quickly got over the curtains in the latrines. Got used to the smell and sounds and flashes of groins and buttocks. To the communal showers. To the rooms crowded with bunk beds, and walls that did not touch the ceiling. To the thin blankets and thin mattresses and all that squeaky metal. To the shared musk and steam. To looking the other way if, say, one of them teared up at the mention of a dog, or threw a can of baked beans against a wall in a fit.

Sometimes he'd imagine a flutter of white curtains. Stripes of sunshine. A controlled brightness. Sometimes he'd trace in his mind the exact, short walk from wherever he was to the locked cutlery drawers in the kitchen.

When they received a message in a canister, the thump of its arrival was muffled by a cut of thick felt on the tube's lid. There was felt on the handles, too. It was impressive, the pneumatic efficiency of such a system. But what bothered him most was quantifying the hair needed for such a small patch of felt. He developed kinship for such compression. He made a point of never lingering when retrieving anything from there. Softness like that could lead anyone astray, here.

The red chair was close to the door, and the door gave way to the corridor. There was always a corner to be turned. Architectural restlessness, a design for continuous movement. No room was a cul-de-sac. This made deciding where to put the dead hard, at first. A room at the end of a corridor would have been handy. Something final. There was no such room. No dead ends, only dead men. Although there were not that many of them, to be fair. One, quite at the beginning. A razor and a significant mess. Much tutting ensued. Two or three more a bit later. Bad case of food poisoning. Nasty and drawn out. You could not speak of relief when you zipped up the body in the tarpaulin. It all had to be dignified and clean. A storage room was emptied and assigned the role of improvised mortuary. They all dreaded the smell, but it eventually subsided. Or the tarp and the thick walls contained it well. Or they did not notice anymore. It had been a long time, anyway.

Everyone was to die, sooner or later. He used this fact as an ointment. He rubbed it on the persistence of bed springs on insomniac nights, on the eyelids of the sick, on the memories festering despite his best efforts. It put things into perspective. It bridged the before and the now. The inside and the outside. Those who obeyed when called for duty, and those who could not.

Feeling extravagant, his mother had once taken him to a big museum in London. Maybe it was the military regalia she wanted him to see, thinking of his father. Alas, he had already known then that grandness had no effect on him. He realised, too, that this was the type of flaw you kept to yourself. He walked in silence, display after display, looking up to his mother every now and then to see if he should seem particularly impressed before a given helmet or bas-relief. He did remember, inexplicably, the Victorian mourning jewellery. Small rings (very small, made for very small hands) with minuscule braiding of mousey hair. As if loss was always to wrap itself around your finger. What must it be like to carry a bit of the dead with you? He had not carried anyone, dead or alive, for a really long time.

In the moment of silence, early on, some of the men broke down. The children, the children came up often in the beginning. Mercifully, the beginning ended quickly. He hoped all ends were swift, although he knew otherwise. The beginning gave way to the now, and in contrast, the now had stretched for a long time, suspended.

He was profoundly embarrassed when he caught himself dragging the chair across the maroon vinyl floor. Quietly. Tiny bit by tiny bit. Every day a bit further. Right up to the door. Then, all of a sudden, along the corridor and into the room with the dead in their tarp bundles.

Grief is a strange one, one of the older men had told him. It looks different on everyone. When my father died I could not stop laughing, he said. You cannot let the body take over, though. Imagine, imagine if we just did whatever we wanted all the time, the older man said, smoking.

He knew it was not good, him in that room with the dead and

the pretty red chair. Not good at all. And yet, he knew other things too. That the room had a door, for example. That no one would think of looking for him there. That he would not need much time at all. That the red was pretty. That there was something like intention in the way the fabric hung. That it had been a really long time, indeed.

Telephone Exchange

Helena Hunter

stand and imagine

you see

the worst

for what exactly

tell the time

funeral vehicle

for purpose

the wait

marks

is it still

the long breath

not sharp *enough*

our voices

messages

is the blue

the only one

sounding

we are the slow implosion

domesticity

rehearsal yet

why won't they

it is a quick

fit

is it worth

emergency water

the weather

occupied

a pencil

can they hear

will they hang our

on hooks

bottle

in here

Tape Relay Centre

Helena Hunter

something is growing
         hear
petals folding
their plans
spores growing
on windows
lichen forming
the shape
of numbers
on unhinged
doors

here messages
are physical
the gaps
reading material
caught within
the vacuum
of private
keep out

hear

    the pressure
of stolen clocks
circling the walls
out of time
       acoustic
unthinkable
forms are
necessary

. -. -..

Fissures and Fusionelles

Delphine Grass

We descend to the basement floor, which I assume to be the safest place in the building. But the War Rooms are a shelter in name only. Built in the 1950s to withstand an attack by an atomic weapon, the hydrogen bomb developed by the end of that decade likely rendered these thick concrete walls obsolete. From fission to fusion, the War Rooms' protection became a narrative spell.

Inside the War Rooms, I feel a little chill. I think how the temperature in the British Library is always very low in order to preserve the books. Within the space of archives, life becomes a posthumous enterprise: a last hurdle towards objectification. In some ways, the aims of the War Rooms are no different. Looking at the War Rooms' thick concrete walls, I keep thinking about how the preservation of one thing from the inevitable is often at the detriment of the rest. I keep thinking about how impossible it is to balance the books, ecologically and morally.

If there were a philosophy of shelter arising from the War Rooms, it would conceive each individual as an intact atom, safe from the prospect of either physical or emotional fission, and safe from the fusion that would bring one into meaningful union with another. The War Rooms' philosophy is predicated, too, on a facsimile of human society, an integration of humans into a system of information sheets, forms and processes: the War Rooms are a machine, with parts made of flesh and concrete and technology and paper. It does not so much mimic communication between humans as it contains and redirects all speech into a future that ceases to be human. Looking at the pneumatic Lamson Tube system designed for moving messages around the building, and thinking of the windows for passing notes from one room to another and the hooks for hanging punched-tape communications, I realise that the War Rooms' real enemies are less falling bombs than thoughts and feelings. Everything here is designed to stop you from feeling your thoughts, or from thinking about your feelings.

But atoms are more like clouds than solid spheres. With their variable and fuzzy regions of density, they are also without a precise location or boundary. I shiver and the silhouette of my grandfather emerges. In another era, in another place, he lost an arm (his good arm, the one he used to write with) to another war. War rooms could do nothing for him back then, just as the War Rooms can do little for us now.

When he was found, my grandfather was lying like a cracked egg inside a crater somewhere in a Russian forest. In one version of the story, he screamed like he never screamed before to get the attention of the men passing by with a stretcher. This is the version of the story from which I am speaking now, the one in which my father and my children exist.

Papapa spoke to me in a dream: suppose, he said, suppose life is always lived in the context of a detonated bomb. Suppose we all live in a world which has adapted to a primary explosion called time. Life is what adapts around it, what thrives between the cracks of universal entropy and inevitable decay. But you and I both know that nothing, nothing can evolve as fast as the speed of an atomic explosion.

Papapa lived inside this revelation for the rest of his life, not coping very well.

I sit down on the War Rooms' concrete floor to write: 'The phenomena of nuclear families and nuclear fission are both contemporary to the atomic bomb.' I think of 'fission,' but I can only remember the French word 'fissure.' I try to remember if I have seen any cracks in the walls of the War Rooms. I try to think of the large concrete walls differently: as the cracks themselves, fault lines between philosophies of self-preservation and evolutionary adaptation. I feel an emotional cracking at the thought that if A-bombs were dropped on this country right now, I might be better protected than my family.

It is dark and cold on the floor of the War Rooms. I remember this: being a bomb once and cracking open. I remember thinking, as I ruptured, that I would never be put back together again, but we both lived. Yet we both have our separate lives, even though we were what we call in French 'fusionnelles': inseparable, intensely attached to one another. I think about the failure to think both fission and fusion together beyond the H-Bomb, beyond destruction. I think about the War Rooms' attempt to stymie the feeling of these thoughts and the thinking of these feelings. And in the darkness of the basement, I think about the version of the story from which I am speaking now, the one in which we all still exist.

fall, v.

Sarah Jackson

'The designers were primarily concerned with protecting the staff against the effects of fall-out…'

– Mark A. Bennett, *Nottingham Regional Commissioner's Office and Regional Seat of Government: Historical Survey and Analysis of Significance* (2013)

To drop. To drop from
or into (something).
To cause or allow (something)
to drop. Of rain, snow, lightning, etc.:
to come down from the sky.
Also of fog or mist:
to settle, descend.
Of the heavens: to collapse
and drop to the earth
To vanish entirely.

To come down from an upright position,
typically suddenly and unintentionally.
To happen to a person; to befall.
Of anger, vengeance, punishment:
to be sent down by God.
To prostrate oneself,
or sink to one's knees.
Of a person's eyes or gaze:
to be lowered.

To bring down (a weapon, tool, etc.)
so as to strike a person or thing.
To cast oneself on or upon the point
of a sword in order to kill oneself.
To descend from a state
of moral rectitude, virtue, or grace.
To be cast down or brought
to nothing.

To stumble into a pit, hole, or the like.
Of a feeling, condition, or state
(typically one with negative connotations,
as depression, fear, disease, silence, sleep):
to begin to settle on a person or place.
To give birth to (a lamb, calf, etc.).
To sin.

Of something sharp: to be worn down.
Of a skin: to become soft and pliable.
Of a person's mood or spirits: to sink.
Of the pulse: to grow weaker.
Of the sun: to set, go down.
Of hopes: to diminish, fade.

In early use also more fully to fall
in (also out of) flesh. Of a lineage:
to die out. To drop down dead.
Of a building: to collapse
in fragments or ruins.

Of a vessel or opening
in the body: to collapse inwards.
Of leaves, hair, feathers, teeth:
to become detached and drop off.

To come apart, break into pieces,
disintegrate. To fall to (also into) dust
(also powder, mould, bits, etc.).

Of night, or the darkness of night:
to begin, to set in.

Also occasionally of winter.

Adapted from the *Oxford English Dictionary*

Exits Exist

Jon McGregor

After *Alphabet* (1981), by Inger Christensen (translated by Susanna Nied)

Air ducts exist, and filtration systems exist. Alarm bells exist. Asbestos fire blankets exist. Ashtrays, oddly, exist. Bleach exists, and floor cleaner and furniture polish exists, and *liquid for inclined tube gauges* exists. Brick walls exist. Bricks exist, and mortar exists. Caustic soda exists, burning through the packaging, which only barely exists, and pooling on the floor. Chairs exist, with wooden arms and foam padding which has hardened and crumbles to the touch. Concrete exists. Crockery exists, stacked high enough for four hundred and thirty-six people. Cutlery exists, four hundred and thirty-six forks and four hundred and thirty-six knives and four hundred and thirty-six spoons exist. Desks and tables and filing cabinets exist. Doors exist. Doors in the drawings of home-made shelters exist. Doors taken down and propped against the walls in drawings of home-made shelters exist, weighed down with sandbags and pillows, positioned against the internal walls of imagined home-made shelters. Drain covers exist, and drainage pipes exist. Exit routes for the drainage pipes exist. Exits exist. Fan-belts and camshafts and motors exist. Filing cabinets with card labels exist. Filing systems for the wiring diagrams and the generator repair sheets and the instructions for the air filtration unit exist. Gas fan motors exist. Gauges with needles and numbers and clean glass faces exist. Glass exists. Grease guns exist. Grease nipples exist. Handrails exist, and the shafts and voids beyond the handrails exist. Heavy steel blast doors exist, with mechanisms that wind shut like a safe or a vault. Heavy wooden fire doors exist. Images of the home-made shelters exist. Ladders exist, and hatches. Light fittings with missing fluorescent tubes and plastic honeycomb baffles exist. Lists of names exist, and the selection of those names exists. Maps exist. Metal bunkbeds exist, arranged in close pairs, in rooms tightly packed along either side of narrow corridors, stripped of mattresses or bedding. Metal cupboard doors exist. Metal light switches exist, pocked with rust and discoloured. Metallic electrical conduit exists, screwed to the wall and connected by circular nodal points in a complex building-wide circuit. Mirrors exist. Noise-dampening panels exist, and carpet exists, and microphones exist. Numbered rooms exist. Office bedrooms exist, with a desk and a bed and mirror and a lamp, arranged around a central meeting hall. Peeling paint exists. Pipes exist, and pipe-elbows and pipe-clips and pipe soldering and the plastic sleeving that protects pipes as they enter and exit solid brick or concrete walls all exist. Plans and diagrams for electrical circuits and other systems exist. Pneumatic tubes exist, with valves and flaps, and a system for using the tubes to pass messages exists. Printed lists of allocated spaces exist, and the idea of allocation exists, and the chosen and the unchosen exist; the idea of the ark exists. Riveted steelwork around boxed air-ducting and air filtration systems exists. Rivets exist. Runs of linoleum flooring exist, crumbling and worn through to the webbing underlay. Sand and cement and water in the vast quantities needed to pour these walls once existed and were brought here and now concrete exists. Shelters exist. Sick bays exist. Signs exist, with the names and numbers of rooms and the names and numbers of corridors. Sliding Damper No 2 exists. Something red and corrosive and seeping exists, behind a door. Tea urns exist. Telex tape exists, and the hooks on which to hang the telex messages exist. The idea of a safe exists. The idea of a vault. The idea of air filtration systems and water filtration and decontamination. The idea of being sealed inside exists. The idea of being sealed outside. The idea of decontamination exists and the idea of survival exists. The idea of the office bedroom exists, the stud-wall partitions removed and marked out in tape on the floor, like a stage set, the furniture removed and the doors left propped against the wall; the idea or the performance of the office bedroom exists. The idea that nothing exists beyond the concrete and the steel exists. The manufacturer's warranty for the refrigeration unit exists, and is still on the shelf of the unused refrigeration unit in the unused kitchen built to feed four hundred and thirty-six people in the adjacent windowless dining room, and has been invalidated by not being filled out with the purchaser's details and returned to the head office in Blythe Bridge, Staffordshire. The head office in Blythe Bridge no longer exists. Underlay exists, webbed and crumbling, and resin bond exists. Walls made of concrete exist, and floors made of concrete and ceilings made of concrete and a roof made of concrete and an external blast curtain made of concrete all exist and will exist and will exist and will exist. Walls of concrete four feet thick exist. Ways out exist.

About the Authors

Zayneb Allak is the author of *Keine Angst* (New Walk Editions, 2017). A Senior Lecturer in Creative Writing at Edge Hill University, her poetry and fiction explore notions of the uncanny.

Anthony Cropper has published two novels and a collection of short stories. He is the recipient of the BBC Alfred Bradley Award for Radio Drama. His latest book, *The Accidental Memoir* (co-written with Eve Makis), was published by HarperCollins in 2018.

Hannah Cooper-Smithson is a poet from Nottingham with a PhD in Creative-Critical Writing from Nottingham Trent University. She was longlisted for the Rebecca Swift Women Poets' Prize 2020 and was shortlisted for the Manchester Poetry Prize in the same year.

Daniel Cordle is a writer and researcher. With a background in higher education and in work with cultural and heritage organisations, he is an internationally renowned expert on the culture and history of the nuclear age, on which he has published extensively.

Ailbhe Darcy is the author of several collections of poetry, including *Insistence* (Bloodaxe 2018), which won Wales Book of the Year and the Pigott Prize for Poetry. She is Reader in Creative Writing at Cardiff University.

Jay Gao is a poet from Edinburgh living in New York City. His recent books include *Bark, Archive, Splinter* (Out-Spoken Press, 2024) and *Imperium* (Carcanet, 2022).

Maria Gil Ulldemolins is a writer and artistic researcher at Hasselt University, Belgium. Her work focuses on architectural interiors, soft materials, and performative writing. She co-founded the experimental peer-reviewed/academic journal *Passage*.

Delphine Grass is a writer and translator. A Senior Lecturer at Lancaster University, her publications include three bilingual poetry chapbooks: *Feuilles Doubles* (2017), *La Traversée* (2013) and *Oyster, Oyster!* (2013).

Martine Hamilton Knight is a professional architectural photographer, Fellow of the Royal Photographic Society and Senior Lecturer at Nottingham Trent University. With images published worldwide, she is also the author of *Photography for Architects* (Routledge), shortlisted for The Architectural Book Awards 2024.

Jonathan Hogg is Senior Lecturer in Twentieth-Century History at the University of Liverpool, who specialises in the cultural and social history of British nuclear mobilisation. He is currently working on an oral history of British Nuclear Test Veterans.

Helena Hunter is an artist and writer currently completing a PhD in Creative-Critical Writing at Nottingham Trent University. Her poems have been published in *Contemporary Journal*, *MAP Magazine* and *Reliquiae*. She has a collaborative practice, Matterlurgy, with sound artist Mark Peter Wright.

Sarah Jackson is a writer, curator and critic. Winner of the Seamus Heaney Prize for Poetry and BBC New Generation Thinker, she is currently a Vice Chancellor's Fellow at Northumbria University.

Philip Leonard is Professor of Literature at Nottingham Trent University, where he specialises in twentieth century and contemporary literature and theory. His most recent book is *Orbital Poetics: Literature, Theory, World* (2019) and he is currently writing about space and environmentalism.

Jon McGregor is a prize-winning novelist and short story writer. He is Professor of Creative Writing at the University of Nottingham, where he edits *The Letters Page*, a literary journal in letters.

Andrew Taylor is a poet and Senior Lecturer at Nottingham Trent University. His fourth collection of poetry, *European Hymns*, was published by Shearsman Books in September 2024.

Acknowledgements

We are immensely grateful to the following, without whom this book would not have been possible.

The Institute for Knowledge Exchange Practice and the Centre for Research in Literature, Linguistics and Culture at Nottingham Trent University provided funding for the Nottingham War Rooms: A Creative Archive project. Craig Cameron of Hamilton Russell first introduced us to the War Rooms and has been supportive of our work there ever since. Hamilton Russell also provided financial and other support for the project. Parmi Uppal, Estates Manager at Homes England, who has herself played an important role in the bunker's recent history, was energetic and helpful in facilitating the writing workshop at the bunker, going above and beyond in providing access and making us feel welcome. We're grateful, too, to Derek Foote, of WJM Services, who helped set up for the writing workshop and who also provided assistance during other visits.

Other organisations with whom we've dealt and who've been supportive, include: CPMG Architects, East Midlands Homes, Marketing Nottingham and Nottinghamshire, Broadway and Base 51. We're grateful to Sharon Monteith, who supported the Creative Archive project from the start, and to Philip Leonard, who not only ran with it, but also shepherded it to its conclusion.

Participants in the writing workshop at the War Rooms shaped our understanding of the bunker and generously explored with us the creative possibilities of the site: Zayneb Allak, Madeleine Burt, Hannah Cooper-Smithson, Holly Corfield Carr, Anthony Cropper, Ailbhe Darcy, Jay Gao, Maria Gil Ulldemolins, Lucy Grace, Delphine Grass, Jonathan Hogg, Helena Hunter, Steve Katon, Michael Malay, Jon McGregor, Ian Sanders, and Andrew Taylor. The architectural photographer Martine Hamilton Knight explored the site alongside us and gave us permission to reproduce her beautiful photographs here.

Ross Bradshaw and Kate Templar at Five Leaves showed immense trust in this project and their patience and expertise were integral in bringing it to fruition.